TEACHING PRIMARY SCIENCE

Aerial models

GW00514740

Dorothy Diamond

A Chelsea College Project sponsored by the Nuffield Foundation and the Social Science Research Council

Published for Chelsea College, University of London, by Macdonald Educational, London and Milwaukee

First published in Great Britain 1978 by
Macdonald Educational Ltd
Holywell House, Worship Street
London EC2A 2EN

Macdonald-Raintree Inc
205 W. Highland Avenue
Milwaukee, Wisconsin 53203

Reprinted 1979

ISBN 0 356 05074 2

Library of Congress Catalog Card Number
77-82978

Filmset by Oliver Burridge Filmsetting Ltd

Made and printed by
Morrison & Gibb Ltd, London and Edinburgh

Project team :   College Curriculum Science Studies

Project organizer: John Bird

Team members: Dorothy Diamond
                 Keith Geary
                 Don Plimmer
                 Ed Catherall

Evaluators: Ted Johnston
                 Tom Robertson

Editors :
Keith Anderson
Penny Butler
Macdonald Educational

with the assistance of
Nuffield Foundation Science Teaching Project
Publications Department

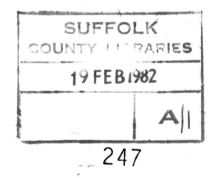

General Preface

The books published under the series title Teaching Primary Science are the work of the College Curriculum Science Studies project. This project is sponsored jointly by the Nuffield Foundation and the Social Science Research Council.

Although the College Curriculum Science Studies materials have been produced with the teacher without any experience in teaching science very much in mind, we suggest that they will also be of use to teachers and to lecturers or advisers—in fact to anyone with an interest in primary school science. Hence this series of books.

Three main questions are considered important:

What is science?

Why teach science?

How does one teach science?

A very broad view is taken of teacher training. Training does not, and should not, stop once an in-service or college course has been completed, but can and does take place on a self-help basis in the classroom. In each context, however, we consider that it works best through the combined effects of:

1 Science Science activities studied practically at the teacher's level before use in class.

2 Children Observation of children's scientific activities and their responses to particular methods of teaching and class organization.

3 Teachers Consideration of the methods used by colleagues in the classroom.

4 Resources A study of materials useful in the teaching of science.

5 Discussion and thought A critical consideration of the *what,* the *why* and the *how* of science teaching, on the basis of these experiences. This is particularly important because we feel that there is no one way of teaching any more than there is any one totally satisfactory solution to a scientific problem. It is a question of the individual teacher having to make the 'best' choice available to him in a particular situation.

To help with this choice there are, at frequent intervals, special points to consider; these are marked by a coloured tint. We hope that they will stimulate answers to such questions as 'How did this teacher approach a teaching problem? Did it work for him? Would it work for me? What have I done in a situation like that? In this way the reader can look critically at his own experience and share it by discussion with colleagues.

All our books reflect this five-fold pattern of experiences, although there are differences of emphasis. For example, some lay more stress on particular science topics and others on teaching methods.

In addition, there is an *Introduction and Guide to Teaching Primary Science*, which concentrates on various materials that children bring into the classroom for their own reasons. This book considers these materials in a practical way to show what scientific experiences may be gained and what science skills can be practised. There are sections dealing with specially useful materials, learning resources, museums and zoos, and making exhibitions and displays.

Contents

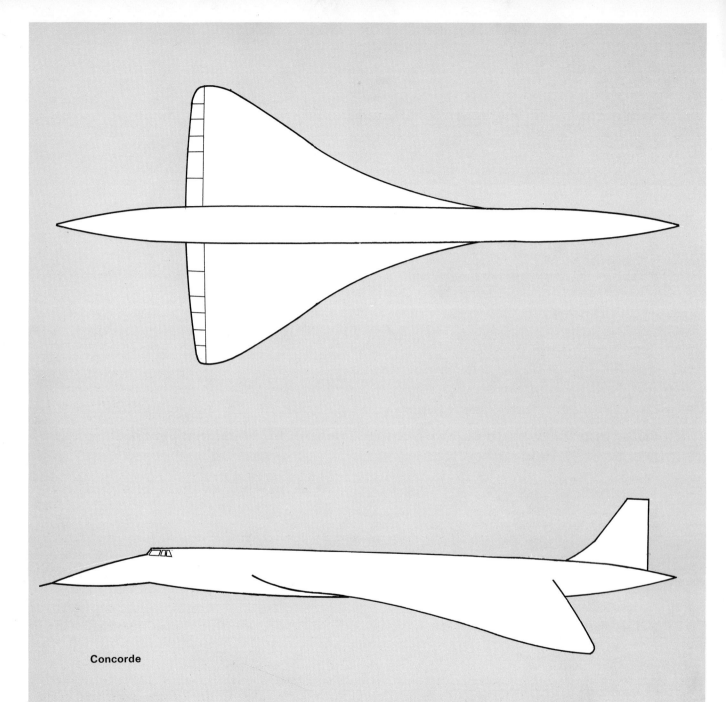

Concorde

Introduction

Children, like adults, often take the games they play very seriously. As Piaget and Inhelder say in *The Psychology of the Child,* 'out of symbolic play there develop games of construction which tend later to constitute solutions to problems and intelligent creations'. What begins as play may develop into genuine work; the child's enthusiasm may become the adult's profession. Activities with aerial models can be transformed in just this way, say from folding paper darts to designing a new Concorde.

See bibliography: 48.

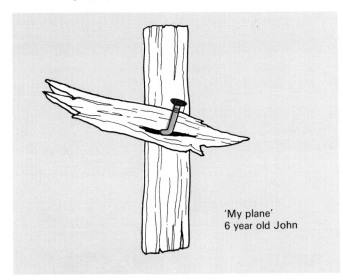

'My plane'
6 year old John

In choosing this topic teachers have many advantages. They can draw on centuries of interest and human aspiration and can also use direct links with the adult world. Parents and older brothers and sisters may read novels about aircraft and flying. A small problem in a classroom may be the enthusiast from such a family who knows it all and has little patience with beginners. One of the great assets of aerial models however, is that they can be completely individual. There is no one single successful pattern, though some will undoubtedly work better than others. Factors which make them efficient can be found out by observing, thinking and testing.

Children's experiences lead them to experiment, and the results provide knowledge. Comprehension comes to a child as he or she arrives at the appropriate stage of development. A strictly scientific attitude is acquired fairly late and may not always be reached, even if the testing of the models is easy and well-understood. This is partly because of strong anthropomorphic reactions—'animism'—towards things which move of their own accord. Just as adult men refer to their cars and boats as 'she', and comment in personal terms on their performance, so in a simpler way children give overt encouragement to their flying models, even if they are made only of folded paper, by inscriptions, movements of persuasion, spoken words, blame, praise and applause.

The special excitement (mainly male) generated when aerial models 'compete' against time or distance, or against one another in a race, has enormous potential for stimulating scientific activity. Of course it also needs to be observed and controlled. The important factors here will be the teacher's awareness that this excitement is to be expected, and her advance preparations to keep it within acceptable limits.

The topic makes a lively and attractive enterprise which everyone can enjoy. The folding of paper darts is generations old; the craft of origami springs from half a world away. Make the most of common interests and skills; some of the children in the class may begin ahead of the teacher, but with a book and a little time the teacher can practise and then surprise them. As with many other scientific activities, nothing here is difficult; one just needs to know how.

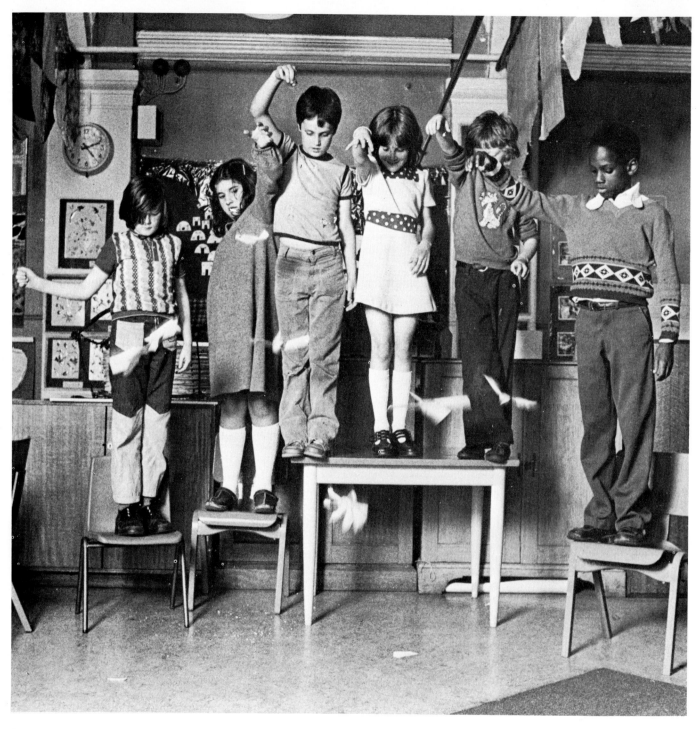

2

1 Organization: people, places and materials

Models which fly, no matter how simple, arouse interest, excitement, enterprise and emulation. All of these can be used as stimuli leading to scientific work, measurement and the acquisition of new knowledge. There are problems however, and these need to be foreseen and prepared for—or guarded against. For example, dart-throwing may be forbidden in the school; the teacher should make sure of the position.

Paper   Paper is now extremely expensive, but the enthusiastic dart-maker may in the course of research into wing-form use many sheets, screwing each one up if the fold goes wrong. Everybody would like clean new unfolded sheets of paper for model making. What do you do about this? The teacher must prevent real waste; for positive suggestions see Chapter 2.

Who?   If the teacher simply limits the numbers there is likely to be an imbalance of the sexes and competition amongst the boys. Can you find ways to arrange teams or take turns? Can anyone join in? Can you keep them out? How do you organize the spectator sport? Can you devise ways to help all the experimenters at the same time?

Here are some ideas:
Appoint some 'marshals'
Test all the very simple models first
Test various factors in turn
Keep the complex models, and those which need glue, until the end

How long?   The duration of an activity which generates excitement needs to be estimated in advance, so as to give enough time for satisfaction but not too much for distraction. The actual making of aerial models will take different lengths of time. An old hand will need only a minute to fold a familiar paper dart, whilst a complex glued, bent-wired, wound-up model may need an hour or more. One can only judge by personal testing and knowledge of the class.

When?   At what time of the school day, or week, or even term, will this kind of activity fit in best?

Consider:
The total time-span needed
The probability (however long is allocated) of unfinished business.
The need to clear up
The excitement when the exercise is a success

Where?   Gliding and flight need space—both distance and freedom from breakable objects in the flight path. Inaccessible floor areas and corners seem to collect darts and gliders, so if the classroom is to be used, perhaps tables can be moved to fit tightly against the walls.

Where would be the best place? Consider some possibilities:
The assembly hall—if there is no dance practice or play rehearsal
A corridor—if there is no lesson-change traffic.
The playground—unless there is a P.E. lesson or infant school afternoon break.
The playing field—if there is no sports practice
The local park—where there are no flowerbeds

At all events, NOT the street.

One at least of these places will probably be available, and in most schools there would be alternatives. Many of the activities suggested can be carried out satisfactorily in a classroom if thought is given to the organization in advance.

Direction of flight path   It is best to have the direction for launching models absolutely clear from the beginning. Paper and expanded polystyrene are relatively harmless, but some organization is necessary, both for general control and for scientific observation.

Just as the adult stunt pilot sometimes flies under bridges, so a child may try to fly his paper glider out of the window. It saves explanations and excursions if the window is shut first.

Safety   Children may be tempted to indulge in other forms of target-aiming, especially those whose fathers are members of pub dart teams. Here are two precautions:
Provide a vertical sheet (screen) of hardboard, pinboard or pegboard as a target surface.
Prohibit ordinary darts, and make sure this is

understood.

Do you make these rules with the children before you begin and so put ideas into their heads? Or do you keep the children under close observation so that you can prevent danger before it happens?

Storage   What will you use as storage hangars? The main requirements will be flat space and freedom from risk of damage. Would trays be available, or empty drawers out of a desk? Plastic bags are good as they can be hung up by drawing pins if space is short.

Names, initials or symbolic markings on the individual models are to be encouraged, since one paper dart may look very like another by the next morning, even more so after the weekend.

2 Making paper gliders and testing variables

Three things are needed—ideas, materials and simple techniques (the know-how).

When folding paper children often make several attempts before they get it right, so plenty is needed. Paper darts and other flying structures are infinitely variable. The study of variations in structure and how these affect performance is essential for the science of this activity. So a good supply of paper is vital. Added advantages would be a standard size, a standard quality, weight, stiffness etc., a kind of paper soft enough not to cause harm to a target, and light enough to show differences in performance for small changes in structure.

A good cheap way to start

Decide on the group of children—how many and which ones, and on the space to be used.

Take into the classroom an outdated telephone book with glued not stapled binding, and in good condition. The school secretary will save you one when the Post Office replaces it. Find some smooth pages, and carefully pull out a few, making it quite clear to the pupils that this is only permissible when the new edition is already in use.

Then begin folding one page: down the middle, open it out again, then the two top corners in to the middle fold, and without unfolding, the two new points (angles) from the sides in to the centre line.

Most boys and some girls who are watching will already know what is going on, and the rest will quickly learn.

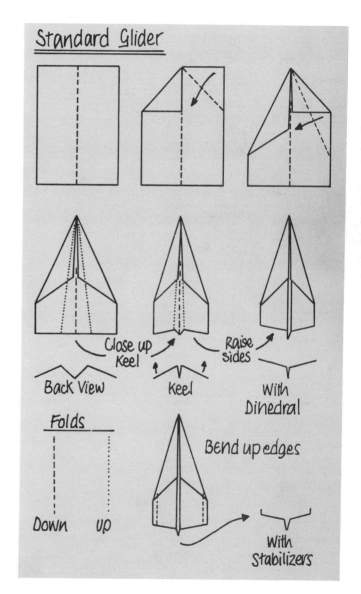

Standard Glider

Close up Keel Raise sides

Back View   Keel   With Dinedral

Folds

Down   Up

Bend up edges

With Stabilizers

5

A very small lick of Copydex under each point as you fold it inwards holds your model in shape. It will now fly reasonably well if you re-fold the centre fold to give the sides an upward angle ('dihedral') and launch it from the back.

Pupils will immediately want to do two things—to suggest improvements to your model, and to make their own. Luckily there are plenty of pages in the 'phone book. Half-pages turned sideways are as useful as whole pages.

Test flying   The vital activity is not folding the paper but flying the product. Children need something that 'works', and all aircraft need test-flights. Where are these pages going to be flown? (See page 3.)

Variables

If the children in the group all start their models in the same way, any extra folds they add individually will be variables. These are likely to affect the flight of the glider, that is they are likely to be effective variables, making a recognizable difference to its performance. The actual reasons for the effects may be obscure; this need not worry anyone at this stage.

Creativity   Children will have both childlore and their own ideas to work with, and plenty of creative developments will occur before any real scientific thinking or testing takes place. However, these developments will probably fit very well into a 'class research programme'.

Working with variables

Variable 1   Each model needs to be tested (a) against its own previous performance—does it fly as well as it did? or better? and (b) against similar but not identical versions. Such testing is scientific behaviour.

Children also learn from their own tests not to rely on the result of one test only; to paraphrase an old

saying, 'Once is an accident, twice is a coincidence, three times begins to suggest a scientific result.' The testing encourages scientific thinking—'looking for the pattern'.

Children are always anxious to put in as many modifications as possible. For example, some of them may add extra folds, making the glider look more like a fan. Having plenty of sheets of paper (telephone book pages) can be a real help towards scientific method. All the ideas need not then be crowded into one model; the variables can be separated out.

Variable 2: length of glider   The length of the glider gives an easily applied variable. The sight of scissors would probably be enough to suggest cutting pieces off the tail end, thus shortening the aircraft.

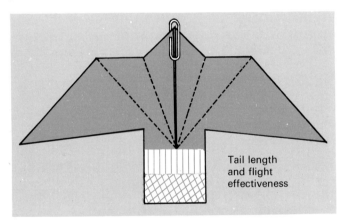

Tail length and flight effectiveness

How should this be tested? By making a successful glider and then cutting strips off the tail end, say 2cm at a time, testing between cuttings? Or by making say four 'identical' models, and cutting different lengths off the tail ends of three of them?

Probably the main disadvantage of the first method is that it is irreversible. One cannot go back and check one's results, and this could be important.

Variable 3: size of glider   This gives a good link-up with mathematics. Start with a whole sheet, fold it into four, and make up one quarter-sheet in exactly the same way as the whole sheets, following the pattern precisely. (A Cessna air taxi instead of a transport 'plane?)

Perhaps even smaller fractions of the page would fly? Certainly a quarter-page works rather well. There is an opening for the mathematical here; if the length is halved, and the width is halved, what happens to the area? And to the 'weight' (mass)?

It is also quite easy to find and compare wing-areas after folding. The easiest way is to put the folded aircraft down flat (upside down) on centimetre-squared paper, draw round it, and then count the squares inside the outline. Halves count as halves, parts of squares larger than half count as whole squares, parts less than half do not count at all. This works out well.

Scissors will give some children ideas about wings, flaps, ailerons and other refinements. How can one best help them to see that to find out exactly what any variation does, it is important only to make one change at a time?

Variable 4: paperclip attachment

Many printed paper glider suggestions propose the addition of a wire paperclip as a kind of keel-loading. This often has two separate functions, as ballast and as a method of holding the folded paper together; if the

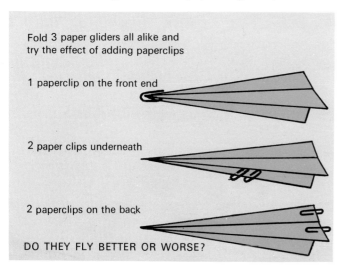

Fold 3 paper gliders all alike and
try the effect of adding paperclips

1 paperclip on the front end

2 paper clips underneath

2 paperclips on the back

DO THEY FLY BETTER OR WORSE?

second problem is solved by using tiny spots of glue, the ballast can be adjusted to different positions along the length of the glider and the effects investigated.

The distance of the paperclip from the nose of the glider, the size (therefore mass) of the paperclip, and the angle at which it is attached may all have effects on its flight.

Small changes make noticeable differences in performance, and pupils may need help to see that aircraft design needs precision of workmanship.

Estimating (or measuring) success

All early successes in flying were measured by the time airborne or the distance flown (across the Channel, across the Atlantic, round the world . . .). The airborne time of most paper glider flights is much too short for accurate measurement by children, but the distance flown may give a good guide to success.

Since many flights are not straight line phenomena, one should perhaps measure from the starting point, using measuring tape, or string, to the landing point, so long as this is inside a 45° angle, as one does for discus throwing and shot-putting.

Or perhaps success can be gauged simply by a hit on the wall rather than a premature landing on the floor?

Scientific testing

The act of launching a paper glider into the air is often a very personal thing, and some children (or teachers) are much more successful than others. This is a problem, since truly 'scientific' results should be reproducible by other people.

Non-controllable variables?

Children's results may be upset by such differences as the force of the launching throw, the angle of launch, and of course by any wind during flight if tests are made out of doors.

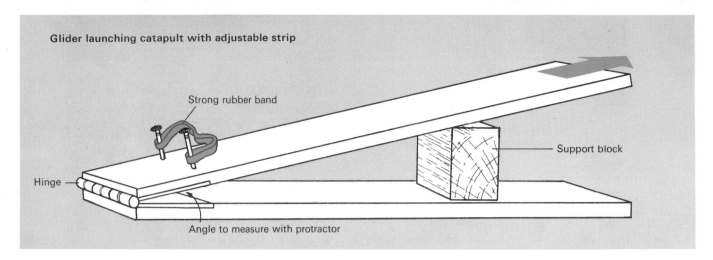

Glider launching catapult with adjustable strip

Strong rubber band

Hinge

Support block

Angle to measure with protractor

Is there any way round each of these problems? Perhaps a rubber-band catapult launcher and a fixed launching slope, all fixed up indoors, might satisfy the most critical young scientist? But of course he or she would then have to think out a possible design.

Even though one may not be able to do the experiment for lack of time or skill, understanding and thinking about the problems is very important, if perhaps only to be expected of a minority of pupils.

Variable 5 Give the glider a flap at the back of each wing, as shown. What happens to its flight if the flaps are bent downwards before launching? What is likely to happen (and what does happen) if they are then bent up?

Variable 6 A very successful one. Try making a blunt-nosed glider by folding back the front about one-third of the total length after making the first three folds, and then repeating the first folds with the paper turned back.
What does this do to the balance of the glider? And what effect does it seem to have on its flight?

See bibliography: 1, 19

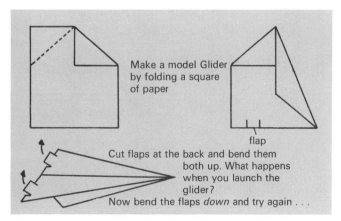

Make a model Glider by folding a square of paper

flap

Cut flaps at the back and bend them both up. What happens when you launch the glider?
Now bend the flaps *down* and try again . . .

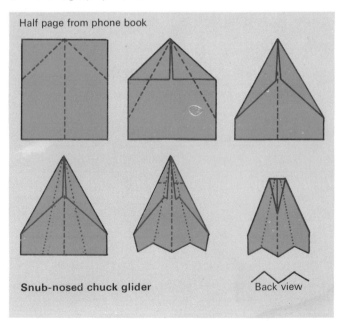

Half page from phone book

Snub-nosed chuck glider

Back view

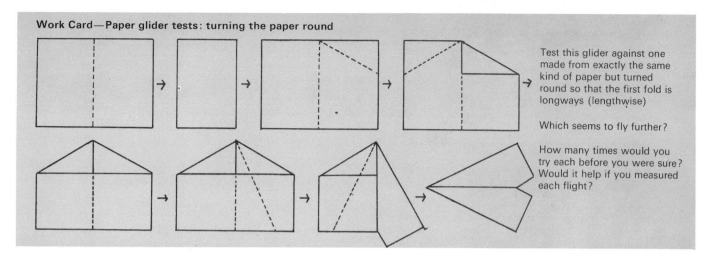

Work Card—Paper glider tests: turning the paper round

Test this glider against one made from exactly the same kind of paper but turned round so that the first fold is longways (lengthwise)

Which seems to fly further?

How many times would you try each before you were sure? Would it help if you measured each flight?

Variable 7: shape of the paper Test the flight of the model made with the original sheet against one made with a long narrow sheet and then a similar sized short and wide sheet, that is, turning the paper round the other way.

Variable 8 Try two, three or four thicknesses of the same paper folded together, thus doubling, trebling or quadrupling the 'weight' (mass).

These exercises demonstrate scientific method: problem, prediction (hypothesis), experimentation to test the hypothesis, alterations if needed, and documentation of the development stages.

Variable x Turn the whole exercise over to the pupils to find the most efficient flier made from their own patterns. Some children will add wings and tails, some models may have Plasticine noses, some will have vertical wing-tips as stabilizers, and so on. Try to see reasons for success or failure, but don't spend too much time on it.

Exhibition

The development of new models could well be the subject of a small exhibition, showing the simplest forms and the final versions, with construction details and performance records.

3 Teaching methods and class activities

Workcards for aerial models

Children who have not previously made folded paper gliders will probably not be able to do so from a quick stream of spoken instructions. A workcard can be used step by step, enables the pupil to refer back as often as he requires, and does not take up the time of a busy teacher. However, the child who needs reassurance most will need the teacher as well as the workcard! Diagrams and colour both make instructions easier to follow and more available to the less literate.

Each workcard can provide one or two suggestions for things to be explained or for variations to try.

Children say they like a workcard with only one main thing to do, and only a few questions. They like to be able to finish a card in perhaps half an hour; in this way they get a satisfying feeling of achievement, and of course do not then have to hunt or compete for the same card again next time.

What ought teachers to consider when deciding whether to use workcards? Some of the questions will be (a) do they (or can they) help children who need help? (b) are they worth the time, energy and card required? (c) can they fill an educational gap better than any available alternative? What alternatives have you? What is in fact your experience?

Making and filing work cards

There are many possible adaptations to a paper dart which can be successful in making it fly. Some children will know more than one, but most will simply fold the same model over and over again. Here is first-rate material for workcards which can be kept in a box or card-index file for 'reference'. Cards provide help for those whose invention runs out, for the quick ones who want to fly everything, and for the child who needs to go slowly with a pattern to copy. Very few words are needed and children quickly get used to the technique.

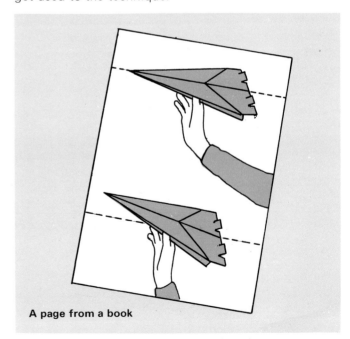

A page from a book

Printed material can sometimes be used for workcards. Some pages from *The Paper Aeroplane Book* would make excellent workcards if extracted, mounted and covered.

See bibliography: 19.

Do you generally find the presentation and vocabulary of books suitable for direct use with the pupils you teach.

Would you think it satisfactory to take a book to pieces in order to use a few pages as workcards?

Perhaps you know of some purpose-made workcards on this topic, with the right comprehension and vocabulary levels for your pupils? You might be lucky.

Children making workcards

Children obviously enjoy setting tasks or problems for their peers; any class 'quiz' shows this very clearly. Children spend so much of their time at the receiving end that this is a most welcome change.

Making a paper dart from a sheet of paper

1 **Fold the side edges up together, making a crease down the middle.**
2 **Open the paper out again, with the central ridge of the fold underneath.**
3 **Fold the two top corners into the middle so that they just touch.**
4 **Then fold the doubled parts—the two triangles from stage 3—inwards again, so that their folded edges come to meet down the centre.**
5 **Raise the sides, by re-folding the first central fold.**
6 **Launch the model gently from the centre of the back edge.**

Given a standard format, say 8 inches by 5 inches (20cm x 13cm approx.) card index file cards from a stationer or the school office, pupils can and will make very adequate workcards, will enjoy it, and will learn in the process. How many teachers find themselves learning new material because they are about to teach it?

Class discussion and action

'Everybody seems to have made and flown paper aeroplanes, but few have set out to improve them . . . (*Science, models and toys*).

See bibliography: 38

Discussing variables

Everyone likes to produce a successful model. But what *makes* a paper dart successful?

Assume for a start that the distance flown at one launch is a measure of success; some darts will fly to the other end of the room in a straight line, some will always fly to one side, some will nose-dive as soon as they are launched. What differences (variables) produce these results?

Remember that children, and some adults, are often still at the 'magic' stage, and only learn bit by bit from concrete experiences that results have real causes.

Ask children in a class discussion what they think makes Jackie's dart swerve to the left every time, or James' dart nose-dive. They may surprise you, but possibly nobody, not even you, knows the answer.

Results are not always due to simple, easily understood causes, but the next step is to test some variations. Two attitudes are possible here, the 'naive' approach, asking 'what happens if . . .?' and

the more technological approach 'how can we make
'. . . happen?'.

In the first approach the model is simply altered, for
example, by starting with a longer or wider sheet of
paper, but still making the same folds. One then tests,
and 'finds out what happens'.

In the second type of experiment, usually proposed
by an older child, variations are made with the
conscious aim of producing a particular desired effect.

Records   Modifications need to be recorded if the
work is to have scientific value. How can this be done
most satisfactorily? Perhaps a short-term 'museum' of
two compartment FLIERS and NON-FLIERS? Or
perhaps three sections: GOOD, FAIR and BAD.
Can one see any common factors linking all the
models in any one group together? Will drawings,
outline diagrams or notes help?

The teacher will often have to drop a few hints to
suggest what to look for, but even so there may only
be partial answers at the end of the day.

Ceiling tile gliders: a playground activity

The modern expanded polystyrene ceiling tile has
enormous advantages over other materials for the
making of very simple flying models. Children can
experiment with maximum satisfaction and minimal
cost or danger. Since the tiles are all alike, some
factors for success may be discovered. Whatever
factors lead to success are due to modifications made
by the experimenter.

Safety precautions   If set fire to, expanded
polystyrene burns and gives off poisonous fumes.
There is no reason for any heating to take place in the
making of aerial models, so no danger is incurred here.
The glue used on ceiling tiles must be specially
chosen, since many glues just dissolve the
expanded polystyrene. The wrong glue may prove
disastrous; find the right one.

Gliders

Whole tiles can be flung into the air, preferably in
the playground and their performance as primitive
gliders assessed. Experiments starting like this are
described in Science 5/13 *Children and plastics*
(pages 46-47), ending with the 'polyplane' design by
one of the boys whose earlier comment was 'you
can't make it do what you want it to when you
throw it . . . if we put a tail on it, we might be able to
control it better'. Many children with a little
experience of folded paper darts and gliders would be
able to formulate a hypothesis of this sort, and go on
to design a functioning model. They are likely to enjoy
testing their ideas.

Ceiling tiles are very suitable for making models of
delta-wing aircraft since, despite their lightness, they
are remarkably rigid. They are almost the only
material from which larger models of this shape can
easily be built.

The tiles can be cut with fairly large scissors or a
Stanley knife; if the knife is used, the user needs to

later modify the hypothesis if it really does not fit. The child who attempts such a project will be able to find the data, and others can be encouraged to help with the research.

3 A similar survey of the position of the 'plane's wings in relation to its body. Draw a simplified cross diagram showing lengths of body-line and greatest width of wing-span crossing. at the correct position. Some people still feel uneasy at the outlines they see daily overhead: the wings seem so far back!

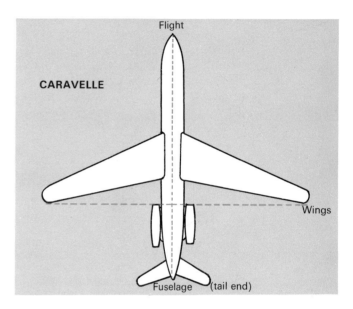

take special care not to get his fingers in the way of the blade, and to cut down on to thick layers of folded newspaper or a special cutting-board (an old desk-lid?).

There is an excellent delta-wing model described in K. Geary's *Make and find out* Book 3; some of the most valuable tests involving a single variable in each case are those in which additions are made to the glider which bring it nearer to aeroplane form.

Aeroplane outlines: a library activity

Outlines (plan-forms) and wing position
Try some of these project starters. Either suggest them yourself or give the children work cards to choose from:

1 A survey of outlines: early 'planes, larger propeller-types, jet-planes, delta-wing 'planes, etc.
2 Attempted correlation between shape and some other factor such as speed. This is excellent scientific method: collect observations, make a tentative hypothesis which might connect them, test it, and

What factors do children suggest to correlate the proportion of body length ahead of the position of widest wing-span? Perhaps speed? or engine power? or total wing-area? Simple cm² graph paper will be a good research-tool, with tracing (or greaseproof) paper for the outline.

A fact well worth pointing out is that it helps all subsequent users of reference books if children are taught how to trace, using tracing paper or greaseproof paper, a light hand and a sharp pencil. Popular illustrations in library books often show horrible examples of how not to: deep grooves made by ploughing round the outline with a blunt pencil (or even Biro).

4 Paper birds and real birds

Origami models

Origami models made from folded paper on Japanese ideas include a few flying models amongst many static ones. Some children have tried the flying version of the origami bird as shown in Keith Geary's *Make and Find Out 3*.

See bibliography: 8.

Group research: a report made after some rather hurried origami bird flight trials
Carol's brother Richard (aged $5\frac{1}{2}$): 'Mine's the bestest! Mine's the bestest!' No reasoning, but he has to compete for notice.
Carol, Bridget, Oliver and Gary (all 9 or 10): 'We think a tail keeps it up/it's better if the nose is heavy (that is, folded back)/the wings have to slope up a bit sideways/if you throw it too hard it doesn't fly at all/some people's throws always seem to work better than others/if you throw it pointing up too much it crashes/oh, and we've found out why the pilot pulls the flaps down at the back of an aeroplane's wings when he wants to land.'
They had turned down flaps on their model, after which it crashed every time.

Analysis
What science comes out of these rather breathless comments? What have the children gained? One could say:

a. some success, some satisfaction
b. at least seven different observations, and probably more which went unrecorded
c. at least four results of comparative testing in team work

d. an untested hypothesis ('we think . . .') arising from discussion
e. an explanation at their level of a piece of aerodynamics; they did not ask how the flaps brought the 'plane/bird down, but were satisfied to have discovered the result.

What do you think could or should come next? Would you consider the skill in making these folded paper models, which they all had by the end of the exercise, was a worthwhile gain? Try something similar yourself, and with your own pupils. Would you have other objectives in mind as well? Discoveries are always worth more than given facts.

Real birds

The paper origami bird may well trigger off ideas and questions about real birds and their flight. What can we extract from a comparison of a 'flying' model with a real bird?

Try it as a class or group-discussion exercise. Make the notes yourself the first time, so as not to hold up ideas.

What things do they have in common?

Well, birds have wings, so have some paper aeroplanes, so have gliders, and real aeroplanes and

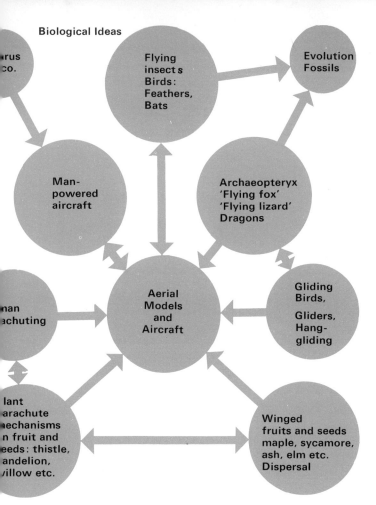

Biological Ideas

- rus co.
- Flying insects Birds: Feathers, Bats
- Evolution Fossils
- Man-powered aircraft
- Archaeopteryx 'Flying fox' 'Flying lizard' Dragons
- man achuting
- Aerial Models and Aircraft
- Gliding Birds, Gliders, Hang-gliding
- lant arachute echanisms n fruit and eeds: thistle, andelion, villow etc.
- Winged fruits and seeds maple, sycamore, ash, elm etc. Dispersal

OSPREY

bats. Can they all fly?

Well, no. Some fly, some only glide, and some can do both. What's the difference?

Victoria (aged 9): 'You have to flap your wings to fly, like what's-his-name who stuck feathers on his arms and then the wax melted.... Did he really get up near the sun like the story says? 'Cos melted candle is really hot.'

Consider Victoria's thinking: she has no concept yet about the forces involved in getting an object such as Icarus airborne. She is however linking up what she knows from experience about candle wax to try to

answer her own question. This should be acknowledged, but not expanded unless you want a very long detour.

Benjamin (also 9): 'Planes have engines—if the engines stop the 'plane crashes.' (This is still his favourite theme in 'free artwork'.)

Teacher: 'But what about birds? engines?'

This is a real problem, since the children have probably never thought about muscle-power in comparison with an engine's output.

Perhaps the simplest method is to help them to differentiate between gliding, which even a sheet of paper can do, and powered flight. Making two lists will help, and it will become clear that birds, and 'planes, can glide once they have got up into the air, but that nothing glides without some kind of 'start'— towing, throwing, climbing to the top of a cliff (as in hang-gliding) etc. Pupils will provide information on ways of giving a glider a start (including catapults)

15

and as they do this they will consolidate their own knowledge, and generalize the idea that 'a glider needs height or help'.

Archaeopteryx

Here is a true story which children will find exciting— they are always ready to enjoy 'fossil' stories. Look at this one: The oldest bird known lived about 150 million years ago. Only two fossils of it have ever been found and one of these is in the Natural History Museum in London. It had big wings, with feathers about 20cm long, claws on three fingers of each hand (wing), and a tail, rather like a rat's tail about 23cm long but with 10-12cm feathers along both sides of it. And its teeth were all round its beak, like the mouth of a little crocodile.

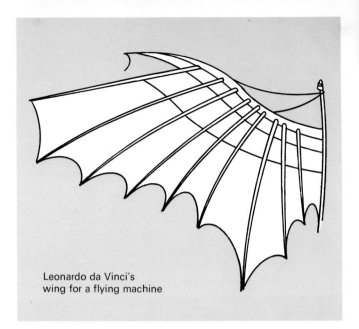

Leonardo da Vinci's
wing for a flying machine

ARCHAEOPTERYX

The fossil evidence suggests that Archaeopteryx (meaning 'early wing') climbed trees, using the claws on its wings and feet, and then glided.

How does this compare with the action of people today who go up to the top of a cliff and hang-glide?

Leonardo da Vinci's 'flying' (or gliding) machine had wings based on the bat pattern, as can be seen from his drawing (above). He actually invented levers with stirrups on the ends to flap the wings, though we have no record of his results. He also designed a helicopter (see page 36).

There is a fantasy element in the whole of this work. How far can teachers use this (a) to enhance the pupils' pleasure (b) to help them to consider the real-life science and technology required (c) to extend their thinking into history and an appreciation of man's achievements? Icarus stands for many more recent pioneers who died in the attempt.

Work-card topics for finding-out activities

(For help with these refer to books such as the Guinness Book of Records).

The heaviest kind of bird which can fly
The greatest bird wing-span (is this the same bird as above?)
The longest distance birds fly
The speed of the fastest bird
The fastest wing-beat of any kind of bird
The recognition of special birds, such as swifts by their wing outline and of swallows by their tails

Similar topics can be found for bats and insects, though with more difficulty. Some children appreciate this kind of 'knowledge for knowledge's sake' and it will certainly back up their scientific thinking. One soon grows out of the Icarus story, except as an allegory.

Further extension topics could include:

1 Study of any available tame pet or farmyard bird, and its special features. Take very great care to have only the owners handling the birds, and no crowded or frightening situations. Pictures are invaluable.

2 Study of wing-limb structure from uncooked or (better) cooked chicken. The bones come clean, are easily identifiable, and can be compared with those in human hands and photographs of bats' wings.

3 Collection and study of different types of feather from one kind of bird. These could come from a poultry farm or shop which sells game birds, or perhaps from someone who keeps pigeons or budgerigars. The scientific work here can start either from the specific qualities of the feathers—firm, smooth, long and pointed, wide and flat. short, soft and fluffy, or from the functions of different feathers— forcing the bird through the air, braking on landing, or simply keeping the owner warm.

4 Wings. Children may find a comparative study of different types of wing rewarding. Birds, bats and

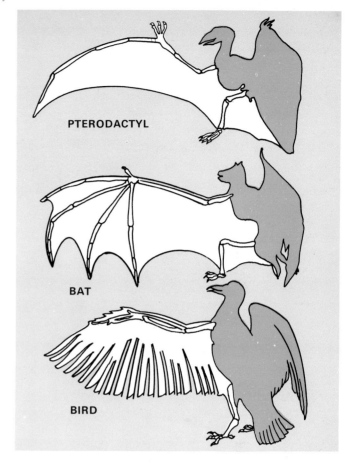

PTERODACTYL

BAT

BIRD

insects are well illustrated in available books, while dead butterflies and bird's wing-feathers can be collected for detailed study. Good lenses and a low-power microscope are valuable, both for information and interest.

How can you help children to look for the separate 'scientific', or rather, technological points which make wings successful? Perhaps by looking for common factors, for example, (a) internal stiffening (bones, feather-shafts, the 'veins' of insect wings, the framework inside aeroplane wings) or (b) an area which is large and flat compared with the size (or mass) of the body.

These biological topics will probably appeal to a different group of children from those who are the

keenest 'aircraft engineers'.

Insect wings—observe, model and test

A good way to practise accurate observation is to make careful models. Things with wings are very suitable, since most wings are necessarily flat, and can be copied with paper or thin plastic. Model butterflies and moths can be made from pictures, so a collection builds up without killing. Matchsticks make bodies, or a glued fold in the paper. Two small problems arise: the front wings must overlap the hind ones, so separate pieces of paper are needed, and moths' wings fold backwards at rest in a soft fan-like arrangement. Use soft paper or tough tissue. Large scale models on wooden dolly-peg bodies are good; extend the slot with a hacksaw cut, and glue the 6 legs (3 lengths of wire e.g. plastic bag closures) into the new groove. Pins make antennae.

Wing skeletons—natural engineering

All wings need stiffening skeletons; insects use elaborate networks of fine hardened tubes. Compare with engineering structures—strength for weight, tubes win. Compare leg-bones, steel scaffolding and sunflower stems. The insect wing network has to take strains in several directions; how does it compare with the internal structure of the aeroplane wing? Model wings can be built with 2 layers of thin paper, plastic bag or plastic film glued on a framework of thin wire or plastic net as used for nuts. Some sacks for potatoes etc. are already made of the right kind of film-on-net material.

Children can see the stiffening network clearly in the transparent wings of fly, dragonfly, wasp or daddylonglegs; a lens is helpful. N.B. Dead wasps can still sting.

Butterfly model gliders—and dihedral angle

In some summers thousands of butterflies arrive in Britain from the Continent; for most of the way they come as gliders, air under the wings holding up the body-weight. Testing of models shows that, as in the aircraft model gliders, the wings need to be tilted slightly giving a dihedral angle—a flattened V. Pupils get good experience of testing a single variable by making several paper butterflies with different angles and testing their efficiency.

Mobiles and balance

All aerial models, from rubber-powered balsa to Red Admiral, make striking and logical mobiles. The maker has to solve real problems of symmetry and fore-aft balance, as does the aircraft designer of Concordes.

5 What holds them up?

Air resistance and force of air

When something moves through the air, the air resists. Adults have enough experience to know this; children may need several examples, the more the better, before they can make this generalization. The experiences should of course come before the statement.

What simple ideas can the teacher offer to guide discovery?

Fans (hand, not electric) Fan with folded paper, or with a piece of cardboard, or an expanded polystyrene ceiling tile. Forget about the air you move, but feel how the fan has to be pushed against the air —how the air resists.

Streamlining Pupils can easily feel the difference between swishing a ceiling tile face-on to the air fast, and then edgeways-on. The easiest way to feel the air resistance is to hold the tile or card at the bottom edge or corner. Some children will want to follow this up; it is very relevant.

Resistance and area

Children can do adequate 'testing-by feeling' if they swish large and small sheets of the same (corrugated?) card, as 'equally' as possible. Is there a difference in the air-resistance?

This can at once develop into a question of wing-surface. Try swishing an open hand, a hand

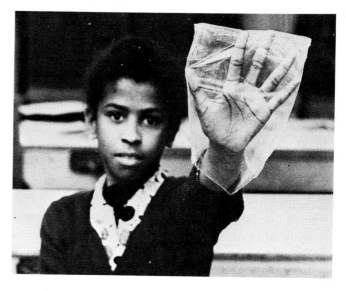

stretched out inside a plastic bag (like a bat's wing), and a hand which has been extended by sellotaping to it a larger sheet of card or ceiling tile.

Janet (aged 10): 'Is that why things have webbed feet, like ducks? My hand in the plastic bag looked as if I'd got a webbed hand.'
Dennis (also 10): 'I've got frogman's flippers for the seaside.'

Consider the next steps, if there is time and interest. What other experiences can be offered? Perhaps the problem of an open umbrella in the wind? The function of feathers on a bird's wing? The areas of aeroplane wings, found from scale models and outline (plan-form) drawings in aircraft recognition books? The extra problems of stiffening and of weight may also be considered, both by those interested in creatures and in aircraft design.

Kites

In the 'swishing fan' experiments, the fan moved and the air resisted. What is experienced if the air is moving, and something is held still in it?

A garage spinner

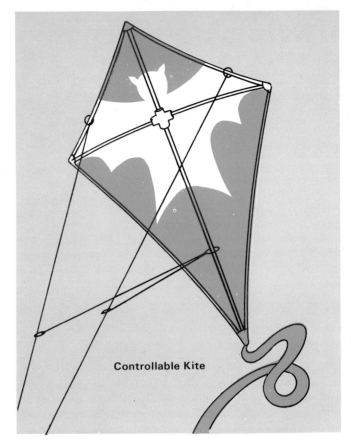

Controllable Kite

Children recognize straightaway the 'feel' of standing in a strong wind. In towns or at petrol stations they will probably know the circular advertising spinners which show the force of wind against an almost flat surface.

Kites, if you can get together the children, the time, the wind, and the open space, are excellent learning material, and very popular. All kinds are welcome, though box kites are difficult to understand. The modern 'hawk' types with feathers printed on thin plastic sheet, are excellent, both in performance and to prompt scientific thinking.

Warning Keep all kite-flying well away from overhead wires.

What about making an Archaeopteryx kite? This fossil 'early wing', part reptile part bird, would not be too difficult to create in kite form. Its most striking feature would be its (string) tail with feathers down both sides. To make this tail you could use two strips of the kind of feather sold for American Indian head dresses.

Consider how children come to comprehend an invisible substance (air) producing an invisible force. The best we can do is to help them to feel it, and to explain it to themselves. Can you and your pupils find satisfying answers, perhaps everyday parallels, to the questions: 'What holds a kite up?' 'Why won't it fly if there isn't any wind?' 'What happens, and why, if you let go of the string?'

Parachutes and air resistance

Make some parachutes and apply tests which you have thought-out previously. Try to isolate factors which could influence success. How will you estimate this success? By the slowness of descent from a constant height? Or by the apparent gentleness of the landing?

Test different materials such as coarsely woven cotton (gauze), finely woven cotton (clean handkerchief) or a plastic bag, all with the same type of load. The load could be cotton reels or Plasticine balls of equal mass and shape, to make the test 'fair'. 'Dolly pegs' make good parachutists.

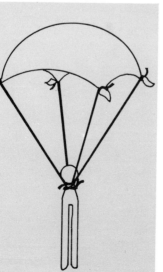

a) Make 3 parachutes with different materials (Nylon, Black Plastic Bag, White Cotton.)

b) Tie equal 'loads' on each parachute

c) Throw one parachute at a time up into the air and see which comes down slowest.

Test different sizes of parachute, made of the same material and carrying the same load. This is satisfactory until the parachute becomes impractically large or small.

Collect, with a class, photographs of the parachutes used by the forces and by civilian professionals. One can see why such a parachute is sometimes called 'the big umbrella', but children could think of good reasons why an umbrella is not a good substitute.

Parachute testing in school

There are problems of organization here. 'We attempted practical work but no stairs for

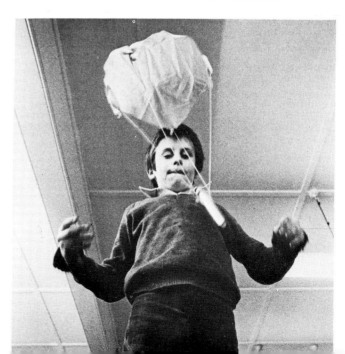

dropping parachutes—highest point was self on chair on desk.' Primary school teacher working on a BBC schools programme.

'Child on chair on desk' would need very careful provision and supervision. How do you find ways to do such testing? Maybe you must do the climbing yourself. much as you would like it to be the children's experiment, simply on grounds of safety.

Dandelion parachutes

This topic would not be complete without dandelion fruits. Children can and should make a careful study of the flight, descent and structure of this attractive example. The hairs making up the parachute top can be seen in detail with an ordinary hand lens.

What can be discovered by letting dandelion fruits drop, blowing them, and setting them free in a wind? They make the problems of the professional human parachutist much more real, the dandelion seed acting as a miniature model.

Summary   Children develop a basic understanding of air in connection with flight as they observe the resistance of air to the movement through it of a heavier-than-air object. In addition, the human element appeals to children, and stimulates them to imaginative thought.

See bibliography: 16.

Shuttlecock and parachutes

Shuttlecocks demonstrate the same kind of air-resistance-acting-as-a-brake effect, travelling, and in particular dropping, more slowly than would be expected

Find a shuttlecock, no matter how old. Then make one from a cork, 4-6 pigeon or chicken feathers and a

Shuttlecock

Compare the plastic imitation of feathers with the real thing

little Sellotape (see Science 5/13 *Early experiences*, page 24). Test both for falling speed, as if they were parachutes.

Consider how useful well-known objects can be in helping children to think: 'Why does a shuttlecock have feathers or a plastic imitation of feathers?' What sort of a game would badminton be if you took the feathers off the shuttlecock?

Feathers on birds' wings provide air resistance too, but a bird moves them and pushes actively against the air. Come back to this point later when looking at powered flight (page 29).

Whirlybird

Get another cork and four similar feathers. This time poke holes that slant into the cork with a pair of compasses or similar pointed object. Carefully push in the shafts of the feathers and drop the object from a height, or let a child do it if it can be done safely.

Children should test perhaps two different angles of slope of the feathers, one like a shuttlecock and one more like a windmill. Encourage this; it should lead to valuable ideas.

Perhaps the feathers stick out flat; what about giving each feather an equal slight twist? Somebody says 'propeller'! Have you a model aeroplane propeller handy? Compare the two for structure.

Drop the cork-and-feather whirlybird, or even better, throw it up and let it drop. Prompt the children to ask all the right questions: 'Does it always spin the same way round?' 'Does it make a difference if you twist the feathers more steeply?' 'What happens if you turn them all so that they slope the opposite way?' And then one child suggests turning two one way and the alternate ones the opposite way.

Consider how much experimental science they, and you, can get out of this simple material. But, the vital 'but', you had to have corks, feathers and something to make the holes ready in advance.

Whirlybird

Get a cork, 4 feathers and a nail

Make 4 slanting holes into the cork and push the feathers in gently

Get all the feathers twisted the same way

Throw the Whirlybird up and watch it drop

Good science teachers need friends everywhere including poulterers or chicken farmers. How many feathers does a whirlybird need? Try making it with say up to eight and down to two feathers. Then make up this beautifully simple paper model. With luck some children will produce one with the strips folded out one way, and some the other. With more luck,

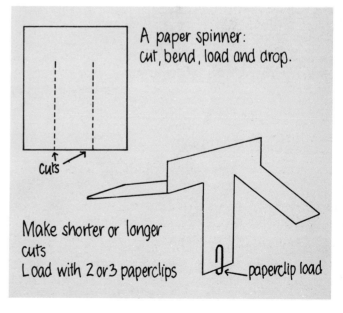

A paper spinner: cut, bend, load and drop.

cuts

Make shorter or longer cuts
Load with 2 or 3 paperclips

paperclip load

stimulated by the cork-and-feather object, some children will try reversing the direction of the flaps to see if this reverses the direction of spin. This would mean making and testing their own hypothesis, an essentially scientific activity. If nobody thinks of it, the teacher can always drop a hint.

Sycamore fruits

The paper model with its two flaps has a primitive 'spinner' effect, and may suggest the paired winged fruits on a sycamore or maple tree in autumn. These are best picked off the tree, since when they are ripe and dry enough to fly they usually split into singles. Observing sycamore fruits can result in a wide field of scientific discovery. For example, children could usefully observe:

a. the structure of a single wing with its load (the seed inside) and its stiffening veins (compare with birds' or bats' wings)
b. the variations in size and wing-shape among fruits from a single tree (natural variation)
c. the relative 'success' of single fruits in dispersing themselves found at different distances from or under one tree. (Compare this with the relative success of different paper glider models.) There are too many factors involved for anyone to know for certain which ensures the greatest success, but it is a very important kind of scientific activity to try to think what those factors might be, and perhaps test *a* few.

Experiences and explanations

Michael (a really bright ten year old) insisted that 'planes are held up by gravity. He had used levers, pulleys and a spring balance, and the only force he could think of which acted invisibly was gravity.

He was reminded that magnets would pick up pins. This he dismissed at once, commenting that there were no magnets in the sky.

Consider this as a piece of child-sized logic. Why did Michael apparently not realize that just as magnetic force depends on a magnet, so gravity depends on something i.e. the earth? It *is* different, to a child of ten, isn't it?

The teacher knows that flight, whether gliding or powered, depends on properties of air. Children often do not realize what air is, and certainly do not visualize it as being 'something which holds things up'. How could they? They drop a plate, it falls.

Children cannot genuinely explain flight until they understand something about air, and the specific properties of air that make flight possible. It is futile to ask children to explain things which they do not comprehend and of which they have inadequate experience. Under such conditions all they can do is to try to give the adult 'the right answer', and this will depend on guesswork. The child is made anxious and insecure when he or she really needs more physical knowledge, and probably more time to develop.

What children can do is to try out experiences and describe what they observe. The more often they have such opportunities for observing and describing accurately—saying *what* happens, not *why*—the nearer they get to explanations which make sense.

Experiences with air

The special relationship between air and heavier-than-air objects which results in some form of gliding or flying can be analyzed by the teacher (though not for direct teaching) into forms of relative movement:

1 the object (parachute, the simplest glider, a spinner) moves while the air remains still
2 the air moves while the object (kite) remains still
3 moving air makes an object move (windmill vanes/sweeps)
4 a moving object makes air move (fan, or propeller of standing 'plane)
5 a moving part of the object makes the object move through still air, by forcing moving air against it ('plane).

Children can be provided with experience of all these relationships, without theoretical discussion.
Example number 5, though the most frequently seen in everyday life is essentially the most complex.

6 Windmills, spinners, propellers and power

Windmills

Find a baby's plastic windmill, or make one from stiff paper as shown here. Ask a child to blow at it, from in front, hard enough to make something happen. Expect the children to see when it starts, which way it goes round, and when it stops, relative to the blowing. Then ask a child to swish it through the air, forwards, and again observe the cause and direction of its spin.

The two actions look so different; why do they both have the same result? Is it because the relative movement comes to the same thing in each case? The air moves against the windmill in one, and the windmill moves against the air in the other. Some children will be able to see the point at once, and some will probably not grasp it for a year or two.

The normal full-sized windmill has been used over many centuries and countries as a source of power. The children may be able to find a small many-bladed version of this in a simple ventilator fixed in a circular hole in a window. When the wind blows the 'windmill' spins.

What experimental ideas can pupils try out with paper windmills? Perhaps (a) curling the vanes first one way and then the other; (b) making two windmills on the same stick but operating them in opposite directions. (These can sometimes be bought to decorate push-chairs). Perhaps (c) blowing gently and blowing hard? This reinforces an important point—that in physics at least you don't get 'something for nothing'.

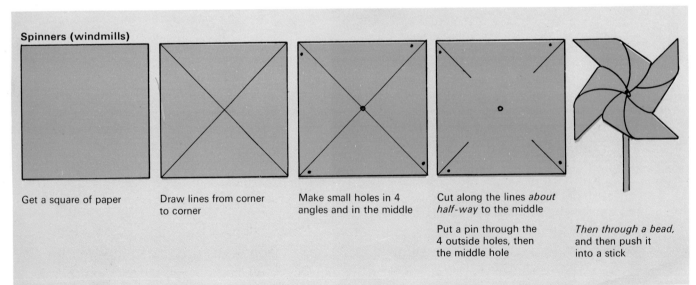

Spinners (windmills)

Get a square of paper

Draw lines from corner to corner

Make small holes in 4 angles and in the middle

Cut along the lines *about half-way* to the middle

Put a pin through the 4 outside holes, then the middle hole

Then through a bead, and then push it into a stick

Comprehension is involved in making windmills or explaining the results. The general technological pattern is like that of the turbine, and some pupils will be very happy to follow this line. They could perhaps experiment with waterwheels in the sink. It may seem a long way from aerial models, but the principles are closely allied.

Spinners and propellers

There is an immediate readiness, and not just among children, to call any two- to four-bladed spinner a propeller. But propellers propel.

One can ask what makes aircraft propellers spin? Have sycamore fruits or feathered corks a power-unit? In any case, do propellers fly alone, 'unaccompanied'?

The fruits and corks do. The horizontal propellers of helicopters are the most misleading of common objects.

Children can easily be helped to think more accurately through discussion of similarities and differences. They could perhaps contribute to and make a list of these.

Propellers and power

Gliders are interesting and important. One of Sir George Cayley's famous models carried a boy a few yards as early as 1809, and Otto Lilienthal was hang-gliding in East Berlin in 1891. These were pioneers but they had no power in their planes to help them.

The first motor   However, in 1871 the Frenchman Alphonse Pénaud invented and flew a 4cm-long model with the first motor. This was simply a strip of twisted rubber, turning a propeller. but it worked. Similar models have been working ever since; the twisted strip of rubber was the forerunner of all the aeroplane engines of today.

Children will not immediately see how a rubber band can act as a motor. One of the best introductions is the cottonreel 'tank' or crawler which most of them know. Science 5/13 *Early experiences*, page 27, illustrates this familiar toy, and asks what effect the number of turns has on the speed of the tank. This brings in the idea that twisting the rubber band provides the power for the tank. We find the same idea in Science 5/13 *Science from toys*, page 40, with a rubber-band powered boat. Teachers, incidentally, need to try these beforehand; they do not always work the first time, and one needs to know one's own models.

Making rubber motors

The special rubber, called Aerostrip, can be obtained from model shops. It is tied in a reef knot to make a long loop, with the ends held down by cotton binding. Ordinary good quality rubber bands can be used, but several will be needed, looped together and then 'skeined' or plaited. Single thin bands are not strong enough. Parcel bands are also good.

Propellers

What does a propeller do? Propel, of course. But how?

Start with a simple plastic propeller from a model shop. Two- or three-bladed propellers can be bought singly, they are cheap and almost indestructible.

The shape suggests an electric fan. What does that do? 'Blows air at you.' Where does it get the air from? Certainly not from inside it.

There are some very small battery-powered hand-held fans used to cool one's face in hot weather. One of these would be most useful in helping children to understand this point.

If a mains electric fan is available, try the following test. The small fans made with soft blades for safety would be good for this.

The fan collects air from all round its back and sides and pushes this air forwards. One can test this with crepe paper streamers, and one can feel it. Look at the fan and see what happens.

But we know from kites, parachutes and other experiences, that air resists being pushed—pushing the air forwards would be likely to push the fan backwards, wouldn't it?

This is a difficult point and needs plenty of observation and discussion. Comprehension of such ideas can neither be rushed nor imposed. Try it as a 'teacher-experiment', and see how well it goes.

Bought plastic propellers

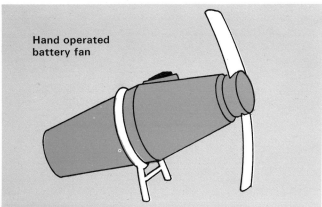

Hand operated battery fan

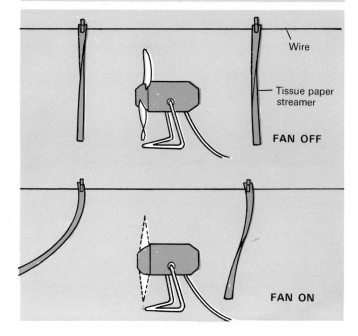

Wire

Tissue paper streamer

FAN OFF

FAN ON

Electric fans push air forwards; everybody will agree so far. But if the air goes forwards the fan will tend to be pushed backwards.

However much like a propeller the fan looks, is it going to be any good for aeroplanes? Well, Pénaud's first rubber-powered model had the propeller at the back—pushing air backwards and the 'plane forwards. This can work, but it is not what we expect.

If an electric fan pushes air forwards, all one would need to do (but do *not* try this) would be to make the blades slope the other way.

Propellers push air backwards
Check by comparing fan blades with a propeller. The slope of the two kinds of blade should go opposite ways, so that the propeller pushes air *backwards* and the aeroplane *forwards*.

This is quite a difficult idea, but some children will be delighted with it and with their mastery of the whole complex subject. Those who do not see why it happens will still enjoy the experience.

There is a large and fundamental slice of physics in this section on power and propellers.

Rubber motor model on line

A model-shop rubber-powered plane can be tested on monofilament fishing line in the classroom. For safety the flight-path must be kept clear of children. The plane hangs by 50cm strong thread from a paperclip, with a loop, a spot of glue and a drawingpin at the plane's balance point. Test propeller winding (turns), distance flown, slope of line etc.

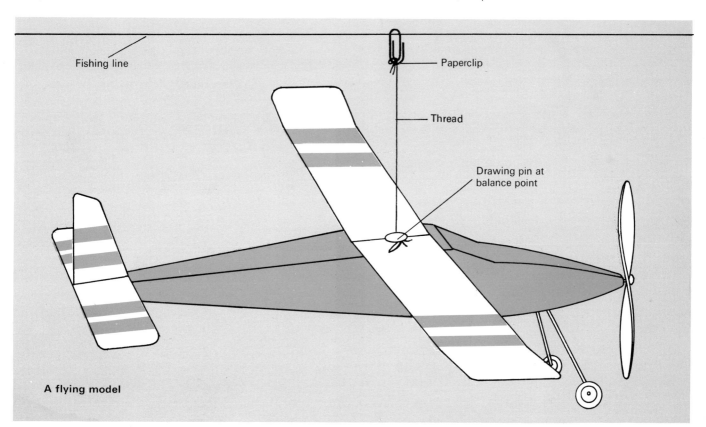

Fishing line
Paperclip
Thread
Drawing pin at balance point

A flying model

7 Aerial models and mathematical ideas

Symmetry

The simple symmetry of two mirror-image halves comes early in this topic as in children's mathematics today. Think of the folds involved in making the simplest paper dart or glider (see page 5). Each fold is exactly mirrored, and children recognize this.

Consider how children explain the importance of this symmetry. Listen to one child, who knows how, telling another how to make a simple glider. Try and provoke the question 'Why make both sides alike?' They can test asymmetrical models, of course. Think about hypothetical cases such as a bird with a broken wing, or an aeroplane if a wing falls off. The more examples the children think about, the better will be their comprehension and therefore their logic in explanation.

Collage Nothing shows up the essential symmetry of aircraft better than a collage of cut-out outlines (plan-forms). When making these shapes children learn about much more than just their symmetry. They may, especially if given centimetre-squared paper, go on to find relative wing-areas. This is a much more sophisticated technique than measuring simple wing-span, and is far more important. Some children may also try correlating total mass of real 'planes, or their maximum load, with real wing-area. Details of these can be found in aircraft manuals from public libraries or try asking local enthusiasts.

Children's ideas and teachers' help

Anna: 'Does it matter if I fold the paper down the middle or across the middle?'

Consider how Anna's question provides a starting point for some interesting mathematical developments.

Take two rectangular sheets of paper and make two gliders, folding one down the middle first, and the other across the middle, thinking about Anna's question. Then test them yourself.

Matthew: 'I'm going to make an airline.'
Student: 'Why not? Where are you going to keep them?' (A practical point, but an unintentional red herring.) Matthew (looking round and finding under the sink an empty seed tray with transparent cover): 'Here's my airport—Matthew Airport—shall I have checking-in desks, and things to weigh the luggage and luggage trolleys do they call them . . .'
Student (seeing that science is slipping in favour of management studies): 'But won't you need some 'planes first? Could you start with about three 'planes?'
Matthew: 'O.K. Then I'll do the passports tomorrow', and settles down to rapid production of aircraft, all exactly alike.
Student (after some minutes with other children): 'Are you only going to have one type of 'plane? Is it the Matthew, Mark I?'
Matthew (giggling): 'Oh, I see. Well, I'll make a small one for important people.' He folds and tears a sheet into four, and makes exactly the same model again, only smaller. He then tests it, 'That *flies*!' He had not tested the previous models, since they were based on an already known formula.

What has Matthew achieved? Perhaps confidence (otherwise why make three alike?) and then a development—the smaller version. This needed *recognition of similar shapes*.
Where would you go from here? What would you think should be the next objective? Can you see a possible way to achieve it?

Area of model parachute

The actual area of fabric or plastic in a parachute can easily be found by spreading it out on centimetre-squared paper and counting squares. Can this be correlated with how long the parachute takes to fall, assuming that its height and load are kept the same?

Measurement of flight

Distance or time? The implicit, and usually explicit, test of successful model-flying is the distance travelled. There is one other popular 'measure of success', the flying time, but this is

31

difficult, especially for children, to deal with. Much experience with stopwatches or sweep-hand clocks is needed, as every sports time-keeper knows.

If timing apparatus is available, it is quite good for children to try it out if they themselves suggest doing so (having seen the Olympic Games on TV etc). Once they discover how difficult it is they may try either estimating (by fast counting etc) and checking later against a clock, or working in pairs, one indicating start and landing, the other watching the sweep-hand of a clock and listening for the signals. One fact they will certainly discover is that you cannot really watch two things at once.

Consider in what age-group 'duration of time' seems to become real to children. Everybody recognizes the apparent elasticity of time, and knows situations in which it seems to stretch, and others in which it seems to shrink almost to vanishing point. Children enjoy talking about such experiences, and can be guided to try out estimates against a clock, such as those of the air-borne times of the class's best glider. They may like to know that the Wright brothers' first real flight (Dec 17, 1903) lasted 12 seconds.

Timing a parachute drop

Timing a falling object, even a parachute, is often very difficult because the time is so short.

Cathy (aged nine) put a jingle bell on her parachute, dropped it when the classroom clock sweep-hand pointed to 12, and noted where the hand was as she heard the bell when it hit the ground.

Distance flown

The average classroom is not big enough, nor clear enough, for good paper gliders to give their optimum performance. Corridors or halls are fine, provided they can be free. Playgrounds or playing fields are even better, except for the wind.

Consider how you can guide children to suggest ways of *making flight tests 'fair'* when there is a wind. Perhaps by repeating the test several times, or waiting till the wind dies down, or 'flying' into the wind first and then with it, taking an average value? What matters is that children should be interested in the factors which affect the result, and should want to think out ways of obtaining an unbiassed result.

How will they measure the distances flown? Metre rules, string measured afterwards, surveyors' tape (expensive) or a click-wheel could be suggested. Sensible pacing might work well enough; over larger distances small errors are unimportant—unless a competition is taking place. The child who measures a flight-path in millimetres is going to need help in any case.

Flight direction

Things which glide are unpredictable; they may turn corners or loop-the-loop on the way. What is acceptable as the 'distance flown'?

Here are some suggestions from an enterprising class of eight and nine-year-olds:

1 Always throw from the same place; they drew a chalk circle for the thrower to stand in.

2 Hold one end of a measuring tape or string on the floor at the middle of the circle, measure to the landing-spot and then take away the radius of the circle. Use the old 'blackboard chalk on the end of a string' method for drawing the circle.

3 Bernie: 'If it goes behind you it ought not to count. The people who throw a discus in sports have to get it inside a special angle.'

In fact this is a 45° angle for discus, hammer and

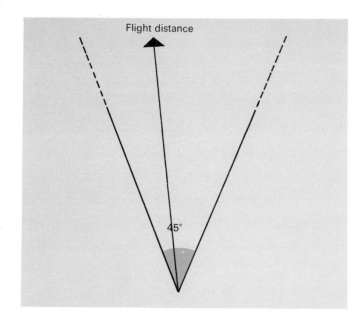

Flight distance

45°

shot-put events. This idea certainly makes the event tidier and safer. A 45° angle is not too difficult for children to organize and mark out.

Scale models

The 'plane models built from plastic kits are usually made to a given scale. The outlines cut out of balsa sheet or made up from paper patterns are also scale models. The figures may mean nothing to children, nor to most adults, but the true size is easy to calculate when one thinks about it.

The same group of eight and nine-year-olds who tested flight-distances worked out the full size of a fighter 'plane from a scale model, and drew its outline on the playground. They plan to do a Concorde, but there are problems.

A further suggestion of theirs is to outline a car-ferry 'plane and then 'pack' it with car outlines, all to scale. They are learning facts and skills at the same time, and neither will be wasted.

The idea of speed

Piaget and Inhelder in *The Psychology of the Child* say that 'the notion of speed' (miles or kilometres per hour, for example) 'is not arrived at until ten or eleven'. Before this they find that to a child, 'one moving object is faster than another if it overtakes it'. Their finds are that children consider the point of arrival and take little notice of distances covered if no overtaking occurs.

See bibliography: 48.

This may well help to explain the particular excitement when an aerial model moving along a line, such as a model plane on a nylon line, actually hits the far wall or end-stop, and the still greater excitement if two model planes are running on parallel cords or wires. Actual measurement of distance covered and time taken seems to be of much less interest, and the method of timing first one and then another, separately, appears very dull by comparison with 'racing' them.

Consider how one can best organize the kind of trials which are most meaningful to children in a particular age-group. Piaget says that at over four years (Stage 1) a child thinks that going up a slope is farther than coming down it, and can neither measure nor be convinced that the distance is the same. This is likely to interfere with aerial model work with infants, since the string/line/wire is usually tilted one way or the other.

Can one try for a dead-level string, or should one leave the whole topic until later?

Maybe just working with this kind of model will assist the children's advance into later stages of thinking. How can they develop their thought without something to think about?

Fast or slow? with only one model
These two ideas are at least obvious, especially when taken in stages with extreme examples such as very

fast and very slow. A young child 'attaches a consciousness and a purpose to moving things . . . all movement tends towards a goal' (Piaget).
So perhaps the question to ask is 'How quickly does it get there?' If it doesn't get there, it has obviously failed, so maybe we should move the goal. (According to Piaget it will not help young children if we move the starting point.)

The line plane model is given a 'target', and this stimulates thinking about the number of turns one needs to put into the rubber motor.

Horizontal (and vertical)

We have needed the notion of the 'horizontal' rather often during launching and flying operations. Children often recognize a 'level' table top or a 'flat' road or field, that is a not-sloping surface, quite early. There are many ways of giving them experiences which help develop the concept of slope, such as discovering that pencils, marbles or toy cars regularly roll one way down a particular slope, for example a draining board. Their first observation of this phenomenon will certainly not be enough for them to grasp the idea fully.

Here is one of the situations in which many examples lead to a spontaneous generalization. This is the way scientific thinking evolves, and the teacher helps its development by forethought and provision of the materials.

Why is horizontal called 'horizontal'?
As soon as children are beginning to get the idea of 'level', not sloping, it is fun to give them lots of pictures cut out of travel brochures which are chosen to show clearly the sharp line between sea and sky. Class discussion about this line will produce a child who suddenly says 'horizon'—and from there onwards the idea progresses of its own accord. Every child in the class can have a brightly coloured illustration to stick in a notebook or file, and the 'notion' is there for good. Is this science, mathematics or geography? Or even environmental studies?

8 Putting it down on paper: graphical recording; vocabulary work

Graphical methods of recording

The topic of aerial models is full of opportunities for graphical recording. Indeed many of the facts discovered cannot be recorded in any other way.

It is important to be able to record the shapes and symmetry of effective paper gliders. By drawing diagrams or outlines on paper information can be kept and conveyed to others (see page 13). Scale models, scaled up or down, can best be shown on squared paper (see page 13). Children learn and practise a valuable skill which they may later use in other contexts. For example, if they wish to produce stage scenery, this is best done from a design painted first on small-squared paper. Then they can paint into a large square on the canvas what was drawn in the corresponding small square. This method provides children with an easy way of enlargement as well as with practice in applying mathematical principles.

Measurements of length are frequent in work on paper gliders. They can usually be shown, drawn to scale, either by graphs or diagrams. The wing-span of real planes, length of flight of paper gliders and length of nylon for the model plane are all measurements too great for direct mapping. Figures alone may be understood, but these never have the same impact as scale diagrams, especially if comparison is involved. It is easy to assume that doubling the number of turns on a rubber band motor will propel a line plane model twice as far. But well-thought out graphical methods show what really happens.

The simple bar chart can be used for comparison of statistics. For example, the flight distances of pointed and snub-nosed, but otherwise similar, gliders can be compared in this way. See page 8.

Genuine comprehension is always more important than the method used. 'Keep it simple' is a good motto. But at all times beware of the facts getting lost in the technique.

Vocabulary, discussion and explanation

In some areas of children's work vocabulary is 'abstract' in the sense that there is no concrete way to help a child understand the meaning. Many abstract words are not within the range of young children and need years of experience and maturity for comprehension.

Consider how teachers sometimes struggle to put across to a child the meaning of a word, only to discover later that they never succeeded. It would be worthwhile noting down such examples, and also those from colleagues, and looking at them. Books which are ostensibly for children often contain words about which the author obviously never thought twice, but which are far beyond the average child.

Aircraft as a topic has an extensive and fast-growing vocabulary of words which although sometimes difficult are connected specifically with concrete objects. On the other hand, many of these words can rarely be understood without the child seeing the

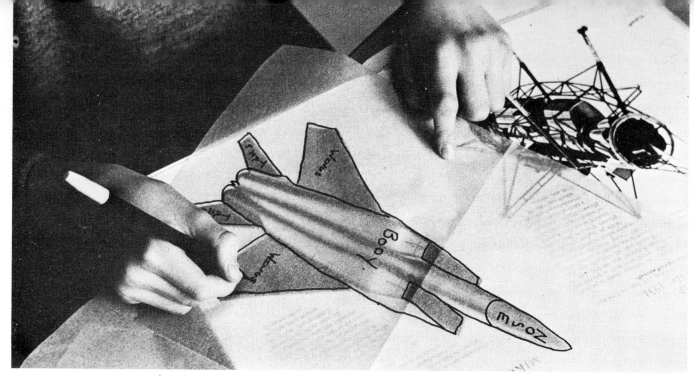

Leonardo's model of a helicopter ▶

object or a very good illustration of it. A dihedral angle is one such example. Given the object in the form of a model, even younger children understand and enjoy using the terminology; they like the feel of a few long words for 'showing-off' purposes, and can be quite professional about using them.

Teachers need either to read up the subject or to be willing to learn from their pupils, since new words are constantly being coined as the technology grows, and children will want to use them in the classroom.

Spelling

Teachers have here a real dilemma: aeroplane, airplane, 'plane, aerial model, aircraft, aerodrome, airport. What is one to do about this?

One can try to standardize, at least for the early literate years, on air: aircraft, airplane, airport. But the moment a pupil tries to find a book in the library the aero- problem turns up. And what about fly, flying, flight, flier, flypath, flypast?

Derivations are sometimes helpful, but more often not, since they themselves introduce further difficulties. Look at fuselage, the 'body' of a 'plane; it comes directly from French (how is one to pronounce it?) meaning 'spindle-shaped', and what shape is a spindle these days? As for helicopter, 'copter, 'chopper', the tendency is always to divide it into heli-copter, whereas the meaning of the word when split into two is helico (helix, screw) and pter (Greek for 'wing') as in Pteranodon and Archaeopteryx.

Names and illustrations

Many constructed names for aircraft will be known to the child enthusiast who specializes in recognition: Caravelle, Concorde ('why's there an 'e' on the end? Is that the French bit?'), 707, Jumbo jet, Trident . . .

Pete (aged nine): 'Miss told us Trident means free teef; I fought that was what Neptune 'ad. Look funny wiv 'at one, woulden 'e?'

Probably the only thing to do with made-up names is to try to make sure that those who use them know what they are talking about. One way of doing this is to put pictures or outlines on a collage, with their names attached. Then everyone can *see* what a delta-wing is.

This method is equally important for the names of parts of aerial models and aircraft, which are really needed by teachers and pupils for explanation. Without the technical name it is almost impossible to discuss or explain for example the variables which can be tested in flying paper gliders (see pages 6–9).

Gavin (aged nine): 'I don't know how to say what aileron means, and I can't draw it properly. Couldn't I just write it on the glider? How do you spell it?'

Gavin's method is easily the best: put the name on the real thing, and have some kind of display-space.

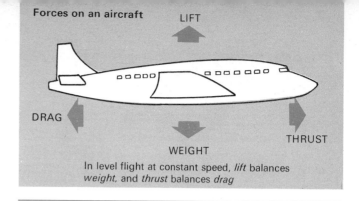

Forces on an aircraft

LIFT

DRAG

WEIGHT

THRUST

In level flight at constant speed, *lift* balances *weight*, and *thrust* balances *drag*

Movement and forces

These are difficult but necessary topics for which diagrams are the only solution.

Glossary

A class aircraft glossary provides material which aids comprehension of objects and principles.

Captain Ralph Barnaby's *How to make and fly paper aircraft* contains six pages of excellent glossary, very clearly illustrated. This is a first-class example of how to make technology comprehensible.

What means would you use here to help children with the acquisition and use of words? What use would you find for:

Lists of words collected by you in advance
Lists of words suggested and written by children, perhaps copied from your transcription on the blackboard for the sake of the spelling
Models, drawings or a collage of both, with names and other words attached
Special booklets of aircraft words made up by individual pupils
A short cassette tape recording using new or difficult expressions, to help the children gain confidence in pronunciation?

9 The sky's the limit

The topic of aerial models is suitable for every age group, and can be attractive to them all. It presents wide opportunities for scientific thinking and experiment, considerable use of simple mathematics, exciting possibilities in art work and display, and for both descriptive and imaginative writing.

The historical aspects, including those daring young men in their flying machines, can be studied at the Science Museum by those within reach of London, while the geography of early and modern air transport can easily and cheaply be investigated from a reference book or two and the resources of the local travel agency and airport.

Science is involved in every aspect and stage. All the teacher has to do is to make the most of it, stimulating observation, measurement, scientific guessing, careful testing of hypotheses, experimenting and inventing—for as long as time and enthusiasm will allow. Some children will carry on the interest for life.

Some extension ideas: technological bias

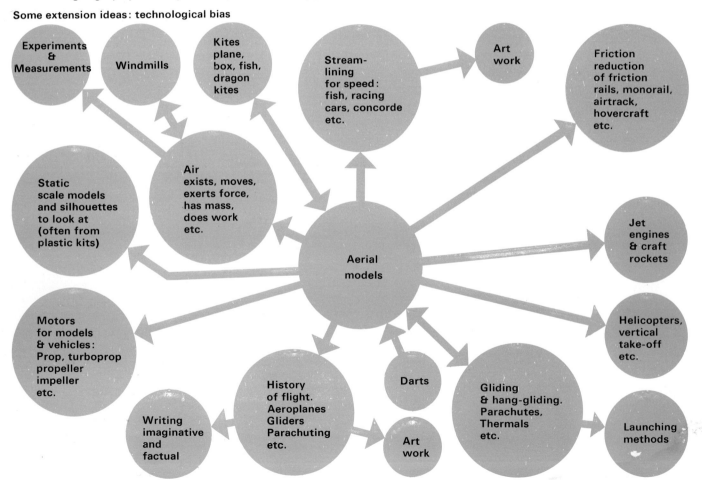

Bibliography

For children to use

1 Barnaby, R. S. (1971) *How to make and fly paper aircraft*. John Murray. Pan Books (1973). First-rate for beginner or expert.
2 Barwell, E. & Bailey, C. (1972) *How to make and fly kites*. Studio Vista.
3 Carey, D. (1972) *Aircraft*. Ladybird Books.
4 Carey, D. (1967) *The Aeroplane*. Ladybird Books.
5 Chinn, P. G. F. (1968) *All about model aircraft*. Model and Allied Publications.
6 Coombs, R. & de Vere, N. (1975) *Fantastic Planes*. Octopus Books. Beautiful big coloured drawings: Flying Flea, Rolls Royce Flying Bedstead (VTOL) etc.
7 Fowler, H. W. Jr. (1965) *Kites: a practical guide to Kite making and flying*. 4th edn. Ronald Press.
8 Geary, K. (1970) *Make and find out*, Book 3. Macmillan. Models from paper, ceiling tiles, squeezy bottles.
9 Geary, K. (1974) *Science-craft*, Book 4. Macmillan Educational. Aerial cable-car etc.
10 Gossage, H., Mander, J. & Dippel, G. (1970) *The great international paper airplane book*. Simon & Schuster.
11 Hart C. (1970) *Your Book of Kites*. Faber.
12 James, A. (1973) *Kites and Gliders*. Macdonald Educational. Starters science.
13 Lucas, J. (1973) *The big umbrella: a history of the parachute*. Hamish Hamilton.
14 McEntee, H. (1970) *The model aircraft handbook*. Robert Hale. From toy to professional. Eleven pages of glossary.
15 Moulton, R. G. (1974) *Modern Aeromodelling*. Faber.
16 Newing, F. E. & Bowood, R. (1963) *Air, wind and flight*. Ladybird Books. Parachute, kite, wing and propeller.

17 Pelham, D. (1976) *Penguin Book of Kites*. Penguin. (re-issue).
18 Ridgway, H. (1962) *Kite making and flying*. Arco Handybook.
19 Simon, S. (1974) *The paper aeroplane book*. Penguin.
20 *Solarbo book of balsa models* (1969) Model and Allied Publications.
21 Webster, J. (1973) *Man in the air*. Ladybird Books.
22 Williams, G. R. (1973) *World of modern aircraft*. Deutsch. (For upper juniors).
Macdonald Educational books graded for age-groups:
23 4–7 Beginners' World: (1972) *Aeroplanes, Space Ships and Balloons*.
24 5–7 Starters: (1972) *Aeroplanes*.
25 5–13 Teaching 5-13, Projects: (1975) *Flight*.
26 6–9 First Library: (1972) *Aeroplanes and Balloons*.
27 8–12 Junior Reference Library: (1972) *Aircraft*.
28 10 upwards Visual Books: (1972) *Aircraft*.

For direct work with children

29 Colbridge, A. M. (1971) *Scale models in balsa*. Barker.
30 Hopwood, R. R. (1968) *Science and model making*. 3rd ed. John Murray. (Simple but professional rubber-powered light monoplane).
31 Newman, L. S. & Newman, J. H. (1975) *Kitecraft: the history and processes of kitemaking throughout the world*. Allen & Unwin.
32 Saito, T. (1974) *Colourful Kites from Japan*. Ward Lock.
Schools Council Science 5/13, published by Macdonald Educational.
References:
33 (1973) *Change* Stages 1 & 2, pages 30-32

34 (1974) *Children and plastics* Stages 1 & 2, pages 46-47
35 (1972) *Early Experiences* pages 23-26
36 (1973) *Holes, gaps and cavities* Stages 1 & 2, pages 16-18, 71
37 (1972) *Science from Toys* Stages 1 & 2, pages 1, 10-11, 19, 40, 66
38 (1974) *Science, models and toys*, Stage 3, pages 74-82
39 (1972) *Structures and forces* Stages 1 & 2, pages 70-73, 78:79
40 (1974) Using the Environment 2: *Investigations*, Part 2, pages 9-14, 93-97
41 (1974) Using the Environment 3: *Tackling problems*, Part 1, pages 52-55
42 Sherwin, K. (1976) *To fly like a bird*. Bailey Brothers & Swinfen.
43 Stever, H. G. and Haggerty, J. J. (1965) *Flight*. Time-Life International.

For further information

44 Geary, K. (1974) article: *Beam mounted propeller* Teachers' World, No. 3392, page 17.
45 Geary, K. (1974) article: *Breughel's toys*. Teachers' World, No. 3396, page 10.
46 Pennycuick, C. (1972) *Animal flight*. Edward Arnold.
47 Piaget, J. (tr. G. E. T. Holloway) (1970) *The child's conception of movement and speed*. Routledge & Kegan Paul.
48 Piaget, J. and Inhelder, B. (tr. H. Weaver) (1969) *The psychology of the Child*. Routledge & Kegan Paul pages 59, 67, 108.

Acknowledgements

The author and publishers gratefully acknowledge the help given by:

The staff and pupils of:

John Chilton School, Northolt and
Ravenor Middle School, Greenford
(London Borough of Ealing)

Keith Geary

Illustration credits

Photographs from: Heather Angel pages 22, 24. Science Museum page 36. Shell Photographic Unit page 30. The photograph on page 27 is from the book 'Windmills and Millwrighting' published by David & Charles. All other photographs by Terry Williams.

Line drawings by GWA Design Consultants

Cover design by GWA Design Consultants

Index